Constitution

Kyla Steinkraus

Educational Media
rourkeeducationalmedia.com

Scan for Related Titles
and Teacher Resources

Before Reading:

Building Academic Vocabulary and Background Knowledge

Before reading a book, it is important to tap into what your child or students already know about the topic. This will help them develop their vocabulary, increase their reading comprehension, and make connections across the curriculum.

1. Look at the cover of the book. What will this book be about?
2. What do you already know about the topic?
3. Let's study the Table of Contents. What will you learn about in the book's chapters?
4. What would you like to learn about this topic? Do you think you might learn about it from this book? Why or why not?
5. Use a reading journal to write about your knowledge of this topic. Record what you already know about the topic and what you hope to learn about the topic.
6. Read the book.
7. In your reading journal, record what you learned about the topic and your response to the book.
8. After reading the book complete the activities below.

Content Area Vocabulary
Read the list. What do these words mean?

amendment
Congress
declared
delegates
document
ensure
founders
fundamental
majority
preamble
representatives

After Reading:

Comprehension and Extension Activity

After reading the book, work on the following questions with your child or students in order to check their level of reading comprehension and content mastery.

1. What is the purpose of the preamble? (Summarize)
2. What changes would have occurred after a national government was established? (Asking Questions)
3. Why were two houses created? Explain. (Summarize)
4. A system of checks and balances was put into place so that no one part of the government could become too powerful. Why do you think this is an important factor in creating a national government? (Infer)
5. Why is it important for all the states to work together? (Asking Questions)

Extension Activity

Create a chart that explains what the three branches of government are and what their roles are. Be sure to include a heading and labels if necessary.

Table of Contents

★ Divided States of America ★

Imagine if our government had no leader. What if every state had its own money? What if there was no one to pay our soldiers or build roads between cities?

When the United States **declared** its freedom from Britain in 1776, our nation was not as strong as it is today.

This Percy Moran painting called, *The First Resistance*, portrays colonists confronting British soldiers in 1775.

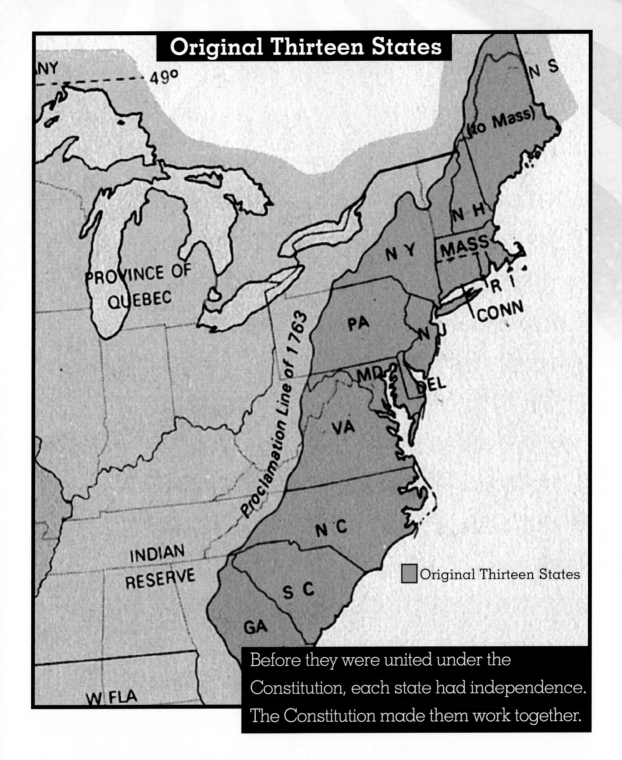

Original Thirteen States

NY

49°

N S

PROVINCE OF QUEBEC

(to Mass)

N H

N Y   MASS

R I

CONN

Proclamation Line of 1763

PA

N

MD

DEL

VA

INDIAN RESERVE

N C

☐ Original Thirteen States

S C

GA

W FLA

Before they were united under the Constitution, each state had independence. The Constitution made them work together.

Many people were very poor. The leaders from the original thirteen states couldn't agree on anything, and there was no president to lead the people. The United States needed one set of rules to govern the country.

Benjamin Franklin, one of the original founding fathers, looks over a draft of what would eventually become the Constitution.

America's **founders** wanted a government that would protect the people but that would also give them rights and liberties. They also wanted to **ensure** that all states were treated fairly under the new government. The founders decided to set down the **fundamental** laws in the U.S. Constitution.

The Constitution is the **document** that created the federal, or national, government. It gave the government the power to pass laws, collect taxes, and form a military. The U.S. government is still based on this document today.

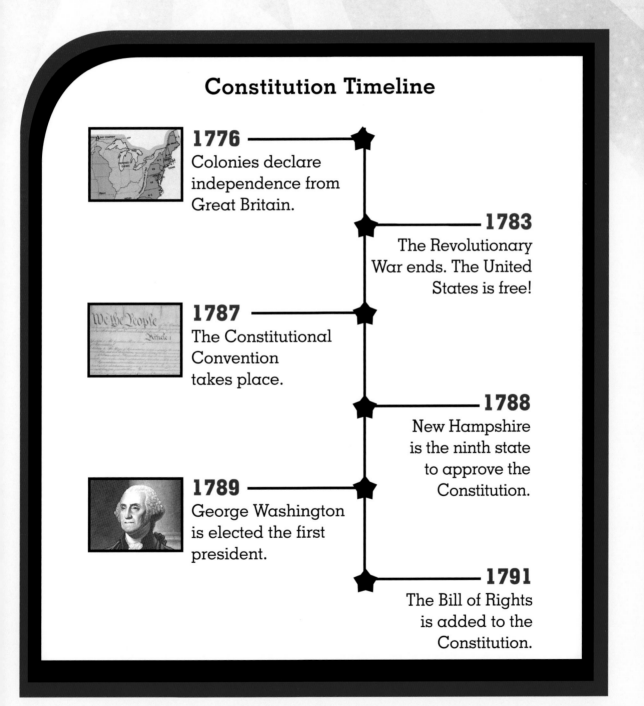

Constitution Timeline

1776
Colonies declare independence from Great Britain.

1783
The Revolutionary War ends. The United States is free!

1787
The Constitutional Convention takes place.

1788
New Hampshire is the ninth state to approve the Constitution.

1789
George Washington is elected the first president.

1791
The Bill of Rights is added to the Constitution.

When George Washington addressed the Constitutional Convention, 55 delegates were in attendance, but only 39 actually signed the Constitution.

On May 25, 1787, 55 **delegates** met in Philadelphia at the Constitutional Convention. The most famous delegates included James Madison, George Washington, William Paterson, Benjamin Franklin, and Alexander Hamilton.

For four months, the delegates discussed how to create the new government. There were many disagreements.

One major disagreement was about how states would be represented in **Congress**, where new laws would be made. The small states were worried they would not have fair representation. The large states believed they should have more **representatives** since they had more people.

The United States House of Representatives.

In what became known as the Great Compromise, the delegates agreed to make a Congress with two houses, the Senate and the House of Representatives. In the Senate, states would have equal representation regardless of their size. In the House, larger states would have more representatives.

On September 17, 1787, 39 delegates signed the Constitution. It became law when nine of the thirteen states ratified, or approved, the Constitution.

With Washington standing in the forefront, 39 delegates raise their hands in favor of approving the Constitution.

The Constitution was written on four sheets of parchment, a heavy kind of paper. You can see it on display at the National Archives in Washington, D.C.

The Constitution contains an introduction, or **preamble**, and seven articles describing the states' rights and responsibilities. According to the preamble, the new government would create a union where the states would work together and laws would be fair. The government would keep the peace within the country, protect the nation from attack, and try to improve the lives of all Americans.

Inside the Articles of the Constitution	
Article One	Creates the legislative arm of the government.
Article Two	Creates the executive branch.
Article Three	Creates the judicial branch.
Article Four	The rights and powers of the states.
Article Five	Congress can amend the Constitution.
Article Six	The Constitution is the highest law of the land. No laws can be passed that go against the Constitution.
Article Seven	Nine of the thirteen states must ratify the Constitution for it to become law.

Barack Obama is the 44th President of the United States, and the first African American to hold the office.

The Constitution separates the government into three branches, or parts, so that no one part can become too powerful. This is known as checks and balances. The first branch is the executive branch, which is the office of the president. The vice-president and the president's staff also make up the executive branch.

The second branch is the legislative branch, or Congress. Congress has the power to make laws. Congress is made up of the House of Representatives and the Senate. The **majority** of both houses must vote in favor of a bill to pass a new law.

The Main Buildings Representing the Three Branches of the U.S. Government

United States Capitol
Home of Congress

The White House
Home of the President

Supreme Court Building
Home of the Supreme Court

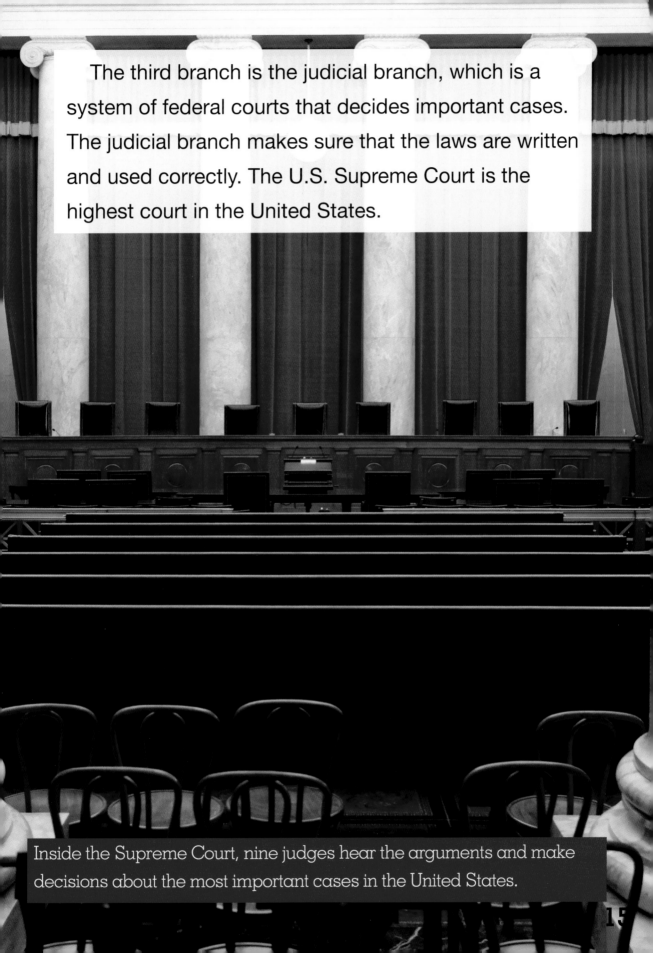

The third branch is the judicial branch, which is a system of federal courts that decides important cases. The judicial branch makes sure that the laws are written and used correctly. The U.S. Supreme Court is the highest court in the United States.

Inside the Supreme Court, nine judges hear the arguments and make decisions about the most important cases in the United States.

This photograph depicts Congress voting on an amendment to the original Constitution.

The framers of the Constitution gave the people the ability to change things as the country changed. Congress can add amendments to the Constitution. At least two-thirds of Congress must vote to approve the **amendment**. Three quarters of the states must also approve it.

The first ten amendments are called the Bill of Rights. The states approved them in 1791. One important right is the freedom of speech, which allows people to say and write what they think without getting arrested.

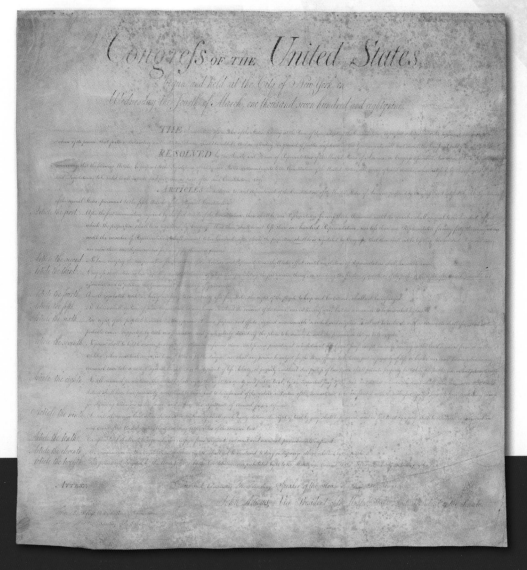

The Rotunda of the National Archives Building in downtown Washington, D.C., displays the Constitution, the Bill of Rights, and the Declaration of Independence.

Other rights include the freedom to follow any religion, the right to vote, and the right to a trial by jury. No one in the United States may be put in prison without a fair trial.

The nineteenth amendment was passed in 1920 and guaranteed all American women the right to vote.

Congress has proposed more than 9,000 amendments. In over 200 years, only 27 have passed.

Passed by Congress on January 31, 1865, and ratified on December 6, 1865, the thirteenth amendment abolished slavery in the United States.

Congress passed other important amendments. The thirteenth amendment ended slavery in 1865. And the nineteenth amendment gave women the right to vote in 1920.

The Constitution is based on the idea that the power of the government should come from the people. Each citizen plays an important part in our government.

The original words written in 1787 have not been changed, although amendments allow the Constitution to grow. Over 200 years later, the Constitution is still the highest law of the land. Today, *"We the People"* includes citizens from all fifty states, united under one flag.

Glossary

amendment (uh-MEND-muhnt): change or addition to a legal document

Congress (KONG-griss): a body of elected officials who meet to debate and pass laws

declared (di-KLAIRD): to announce something officially

delegates (DEL-uh-guhts): people chosen to represent others at a meeting

document (DAHK-yuh-muhnt): a paper containing official information

ensure (en-SHOOR): to make sure something happens

founders (FOUND-urz): people responsible for establishing something

fundamental (fuhn-duh-MEN-tuhl): very important

majority (muh-JOR-i-tee): more than half

preamble (PREE-am-buhl): the introduction to the Constitution explaining the purpose of the Constitution

representatives (rep-ri-ZEN-tuh-tivs): people who are chosen to speak or act on behalf of others

Index

Show What You Know

1. Why did the United States need a new government?
2. How did the Great Compromise provide states with equal representation in Congress?
3. What is the Bill of Rights?
4. What are the three branches of government?
5. Why might an amendment be added to the Constitution?

Websites to Visit

www.constitutioncenter.org
www.usconstitution.net/constkids4.html
www.congressforkids.net/Constitution_index.htm

About the Author

Kyla Steinkraus loves the story of how the U.S. Constitution was created. Many people with very different opinions came together and compromised to create a brand new government. It is still a government based on the will and voice of the people, and that is a wonderful thing! She lives with her husband and two children in Tampa, Florida. She enjoys drawing, photography, and writing.

Meet The Author!
www.meetREMauthors.com

www.rourkeeducationalmedia.com

PHOTO CREDITS: Cover © National Archives, Howard Chandler Christy/U.S. government; title page, page 11, 17 © U.S. Natinal Archives; page 4, 6, 9, 18 © Library of Congress; page 5 © Department of the Interior; page 10 © Images of American Political History; page 13 © Wikipedia; page 14 © trekand shoot/albert debruijn/Backyard Production; page 15 © wellesenterprises; page 16 © AP Images; page 19 © Francis Bicknell Carpenter/Senate.gov; page 20 © Mark Hatfield

Edited by: Jill Sherman

Cover by: Nicola Stratford, nicolastratford.com
Interior design by: Jen Thomas

Library of Congress PCN Data

Constitution/ Kyla Steinkraus
 (U.S. Government and Civics)
  ISBN 978-1-62717-681-1 (hard cover)
  ISBN 978-1-62717-803-7(soft cover)
  ISBN 978-1-62717-919-5 (e-Book)
Library of Congress Control Number: 2014935456

Printed in the United States of America, North Mankato, Minnesota

Also Available as:

ROURKE'S
e-Books